The Liminal Journal

Navigating the Vital Space
Between the Life You Built and
the Life That's Calling You Forward

Nichomi Higgins, LMFT

Publishing Services provided by HypeHouse Digital

Printed in the United States of America

First Printing, 2026

Layout Design by Rachel Lambert,

rlambertdesign.com

ISBN Paperback 978-1-7360258-4-0

"Clarity is often born in the ashes of the life we outgrow."
—Nichomi Higgins, LMFT

Table of Contents

A Poem

As I walk through this dark and quiet space
what remains, what is left, I reach within my heart
and pull out the light of self-compassion and gratitude.

Even in this rubble I call myself,
I recognize the pieces of me that are true.
The pieces that have always been.
The pieces that stand tall in this light
and reflect back to me the promise
that all will be well.

And in this moment,
with the glow of my heart lighting the path,
I am reminded that freedom can only be embodied
when the dead and dying things
have been stripped away.

How To Use This Reflection Journal

This journal is not meant to be rushed or completed in one sitting. It is not a linear experience either. Think of it as a companion for the season when your inner world is shifting in ways you can feel but cannot yet fully name. That foggy and vital space between the over-functioning version of you that is ending and the whole and creative version of you that is waiting to begin.

As a therapist I have always held the belief that growth does not come from having all the answers. It comes from asking empowering questions. Questions that help us orient when the ground beneath us is shifting. And questions rooted in both grace and curiosity that lead us out of the fog and into the clearing if we only give ourselves permission to answer truthfully. Even when the truth feels half baked and a little messy.

That is the purpose of this journal. Not to give you a formula, but to help you arrive at your own roadmap by reconnecting you to a deeper intelligence rising in you now. The part of you that is now loudly declaring that it's time to consider a new way of leading, or creating, or relating or just existing.

You see, many of us can feel a chapter closing. We are exhausted. We are done running our lives and businesses through the filter of respectability politics. Done with over-functioning. Done with hyper caretaking. Done with the hustle and the grind. All of it.

But here is where we struggle. We struggle to name where we want to go from here. Not because we are unclear, but because what is rising is also asking us to release something. *Somebody.* Some role. Some idea, and that kind of shift can feel deeply disruptive.

Maybe because it does not fit the status quo. Maybe because it does not feel financially convenient or fruitful. Or maybe it is asking you to finally stand on business and do the thing you've been circling for years.

This journal gives you space to insert your truth without needing permission.

As you move through these thresholds, you may notice your mind wanting to rush toward answers or fix your experience. Some questions will feel clarifying. Others may feel emotionally charged. None of them are demands. All of them are invitations.

Treat this journal as a dialogue between you and your body, you and your intuition, you and your G-d. You and the dream that is asking to be named. Let it help you notice what is loosening, what is ending, what is returning, and what is ready to emerge.

A FEW GENTLE GUIDELINES AS YOU MOVE THROUGH THE PAGES:

Honor your pace.
You cannot rush a threshold. Move only as fast as your spirit allows.

Write without editing.
Let your answers be raw, unfiltered, and honest. This is not an assignment that will be graded. Return to the questions that won't let you go. They often hold the truth you are finally ready to name.

Pause when needed.
Your spirit deserves care. Take breaks. Drink water. Walk. Breathe.

Let your answers evolve.
Who you are becoming will shift as you move through each threshold. Allow your truth to change as you change. The only rule is that you chart this new path with a level of self-compassion that is fitting for anyone charting a new path.

Bring into your therapy.
Most therapists will welcome this initiative and the insight that can be unpacked and explored together.

Access The Guided Meditation Library:

Scan Here To Access

This companion library is not meant to be robust or overwhelming. It was created with the understanding that in seasons of unearthing, acceptance, and reimagining, the body also needs care. Tending to our energy can create the spaciousness needed to process and move through grief, rebirth, and embodiment as they arise. This library is here to support you as you steady yourself and continue forward.

As a gentle reminder, this journal is a mirror that helps you see where you are — so you can choose your next step with intention, clarity, and a deeper sense of self-trust.

Disclaimer

Throughout this journal, you will encounter questions, reflections, activities, and prayers that are shaped by my own relationship with meaning, truth, and the divine. You are not being asked to adopt my beliefs or framework. You are invited to translate what you encounter here into language, practices, and understanding that align with your own lived experience.

If prayer or spiritual reflection is part of your practice, you may sit with the words offered as they are, adapt them into your own language, or allow them to spark something more personal. If prayer is not part of your practice, you may read these sections as reflections, intentions, or meditations, or skip them entirely.

There is no right way to engage with these pages. Honor what resonates. Release what does not. Your agency matters here.

Naming Your Feelings

Source unknown

Threshold One

WHEN YOUR EARTH STARTS TO SHIFT

The disruption before transformation

There are seasons in our lives when something deep inside begins to shift long before we have language for it. Sometimes the shift arrives subtly, like a quiet tightening in the chest or a sudden disinterest in the roles and rhythms that once felt like home. Other times it feels like a spiritual aftershock, a rupture that moves through the body faster than the mind can interpret.

My own unraveling arrived around my career and the identity I had spent years building. Nothing in my outer life had collapsed yet, but I could feel the ground loosening beneath my feet. I remember ending a therapy session and thinking, *What would it look like if I took my foot off the gas?* The question sent me into a panic. That was the first tremor.

Conversations felt different. Work that once lit me up became heavy. The woman I had mastered being no longer fit, and I could no longer pretend I didn't feel it.

Back then, I tried to outrun the truth. I created new programs. I learned new modalities. I focused on speaking, writing, building — anything to revive a fire that was quietly changing temperature.

I had spent years in pursuit of the dream, the vision, the impact. To acknowledge the tremor meant acknowledging that the structure, identity, and expectations I had poured my all into were no longer working.

In my therapy room, I call this an internal rupture. In spiritual language, it can feel like a calling wrapped in discomfort. In philosophy, it looks like existential honesty — the moment when the story you've been living can no longer carry the meaning it once did. Whatever name you give it, this threshold is not a punishment. It is an invitation to pause, listen, and meet the truth rising beneath the noise.

These tremors rarely feel holy at first. That may be an assumption, but I can only speak from experience. They often show up as exhaustion, boredom, or disconnection. For some, they appear as irritation, anger, or skepticism. More often than not, grief without an obvious loss is present. You may feel guilty for wanting something or someone different. You may fear losing what you've built. You may wonder if you're losing your mind. In reality, you're shedding a way of being that could never carry you into the next chapter.

So this, my fellow traveler, is where your journal begins. Not with answers or a five-step plan, but with the honest acknowledgment that the foundation within you is shifting. This threshold is the first doorway into your new normal.

Ground

Before you begin, pause.

Take a deep inhalation through your nose and a full exhalation through your open mouth. Allow each breath to center you in the living force that moves through your body.

Notice where your body is supported right now. The chair beneath you. The floor under your feet. Let your breath arrive without effort.

You are not here to fix anything. You are here to notice what is shifting.

Affirm

I will not allow my need for perfection,
or my desire to be perceived as exceptional,
impede my next move.

*(You may repeat this silently, write it once,
or simply let it sit with you.)*

Begin

SIGNS OF DISRUPTION THAT SIGNAL CHANGE

For some, the earliest signs of change feel less like a decision and more like a physical or spiritual restlessness; a tension even.

What physical, emotional, or spiritual signs are letting you know that something in you is shifting?

What feels different about this season?

WHAT FAITH MEANS RIGHT NOW

Words, like prayer, meditation, faith and spirituality hold so much meaning for us all. But they are not immune to change and evolution.

At this moment, what does faith or spirituality mean to you, and how would you describe its presence or absence in your life right now?

WHAT IS BEING RELEASED?

You may notice that what's shifting isn't your desire to enjoy the results of your work, but your relationship to the version of you who had to carry things a certain way.

This might look like a habit that once produced results, a role that now feels draining, or a value that no longer sits at the center. When this loosens, it can feel disorienting or even frightening—especially if your sense of security feels tied to it.

What feels like it is loosening or no longer fitting in your life right now?

What emotions surface as you notice this shift?

When you consider your current way of leading or holding responsibility for others, what feels too tight, strained, or no longer aligned?

HOLDING ON

In this season of detangling, you may notice a great deal of ambivalence showing up. Decisions feel heavier than usual. Your mind tries to commit to a direction while your spirit hesitates.

When this happens, a part of you will rush in to keep everything in place. When the ground inside you starts to shift, how do you find yourself trying to keep things the same?

Am I forcing something to work even as my body or intuition is asking me to pause?

THE FEAR BENEATH THE SHIFT

Fear will be frequently revisited throughout this journal. But for now and in this season, when you consider what is collapsing or evolving in your life, what fears surface?

Where do you feel them — physically or relationally?

What feels most at stake right now?

WHAT IS STILL IN YOUR CONTROL

Even in uncertainty, agency remains. Sometimes it is your breath. Sometimes it is the next small decision. Sometimes it is simply the choice to sit with the truth. Let's take inventory!

In this season, where do you still notice choice or agency available to you, even in small ways?

What shifts for you (physically, emotionally, etc.), when you notice where you still hold agency?

Closing Activities

What you have written in these pages — whether complete thoughts, scattered feelings, or emotions — belongs to you.

When you feel finished processing within this threshold, or simply finished reflecting for now, choose one of the following closing activities:

ACTIVITY ONE

Grounding Through Nature

PURPOSE:

To give your mind a rest and allow insight to arrive without effort.

INSTRUCTIONS:

- **Step outside and take a short walk in nature.** As you walk, notice a grounded, rooted life form that draws your attention. Do not interpret it. Simply observe.

- **Notice its presence.** Notice any parts that have fallen to the ground — leaves, petals, or fragments. Consider what purpose they may have once served, if any. Notice what comes up for you. Remember that you and this life form are made from the same sacred material.

- **Collect five natural objects** that speak to this season of your life. They do not need to make sense. You only need to feel drawn to them.

- When you return, place them somewhere visible or store them between these pages. Let meaning emerge later.

ACTIVITY TWO

Considering Professional Support

PURPOSE:

To explore whether professional support could help hold this season.

REFLECTION:

If you are experiencing sustained sadness, overwhelm, anxiety, or a sense of unraveling that is beginning to affect your daily life, this may be a season where professional support could be helpful. Remember, seeking support is not a failure of resilience. It is a form of care.

CONSIDER REFLECTING ON ONE OR TWO OF THE FOLLOWING:

- What am I hoping support could help me hold or understand right now?
- What feels too heavy to carry alone?
- What kind of support would feel safest or most grounding in this season?

OPTIONAL:

If therapy feels like a possibility,
you may want to ask a potential therapist:

- How do you support clients navigating identity transitions or burnout?
- What is your approach when someone feels unsure or ungrounded?
- How do you work with grief that does not have a clear ending?

ACTIVITY THREE

Naming Safe Support

PURPOSE:

To reduce isolation and invite connection without pressure.

REFLECTION:

You do not need to have language for your experience to deserve support. Sometimes, you just need a space to ramble. Or simply to be in company with another.

CONSIDER:

- Who in my life can I be unpolished with?
- Who allows me to speak without needing clarity or resolution?
- Who feels steady enough to sit with me while I don't have answers?

REMEMBER:

When reaching out, always check whether or not your loved one has the capacity.

Threshold
Two

THE LIMINAL MAP

Learning where you are inside yourself

Before you read further, pause.

Place one hand on your body. Notice where you feel contact or pressure. You don't need to interpret it. Just notice that you are here.

This threshold is not asking you to solve yourself. It is asking you to stay with yourself long enough to both notice and connect with what remains.

Threshold Two is where the dust doesn't quite settle, but it stops feeling like a storm. The air is still thick, and you can't see far ahead, yet something in you knows the ground has shifted for good. You may not recognize who you were, and you may not yet understand who you are becoming. But you are taking steps forward, even if they are wobbly and uncertain. This in-between space carries its own kind of vertigo. The sense that your inner world is rearranging itself faster than your mind can keep up.

There is a quiet fragility here. Not danger, but exposure. For some, this threshold feels like an unsettling stillness after an internal earthquake. For others, especially those who have been over-functioning or holding everyone else together for years, it can feel like you are to blame. Everyone else seems to be sinking after you release their lifeline, and they refuse to swim. This adds more pressure to the collapse of your old self.

Then there are those who describe this season as a rebirth that begins after an ego death. These experiences are vast and varied. Either way, the spark you once relied on begins to dim. The rhythms you trusted thin out. The instincts that once made you feel capable suddenly feel far away. With that loss of certainty comes a need for care and support that can frighten even the strongest among us.

Nothing is wrong. This is what it feels like when the deeper truth inside you begins to reorder the architecture of your inner life. The old ways of making meaning no longer carry you and therefore your identity feels as though it is unraveling. The questions you used to ask don't yield answers. Even your body starts speaking in a new language that favors honesty over performance, slowness over urgency, presence over production.

Many arrive here exhausted from trying to keep up appearances or meet responsibilities while quietly breaking inside. Some try to disappear into their own lives, hiding in plain sight, hoping no one notices how heavy things feel. Others reach for help they can't afford, or draft messages they never send, searching for someone who can make sense of what feels impossible to articulate. You are not alone in that experience. And you are not failing. You are arriving at a threshold that asks you to see yourself with a different kind of compassion.

This is the moment when you learn the contours of the new ground beneath you. Not perfectly. Not confidently. Just honestly. The questions in this threshold are here to help you see what is still true, what is still yours, and what is waiting for you beneath the debris even if you can't name it yet. This is the beginning of orientation. The quiet recognition that, even here, something in you is still alive and reaching for what comes next.

Orient

Before continuing, take a moment to orient yourself to the room around you.

Grab, smell, or taste something that brings you comfort. Then…

- Name three things you can see.
- Name two things you can hear.
- Name one place in your body that feels neutral or steady.

Nothing needs to make sense yet.

Affirm

Being the full expression of who I am is part of my life's purpose.

I cultivate an inner foundation of trust and connection to Source that allows me to gracefully navigate my evolution, even when there is more uncertainty than clarity.

I am fully present to all that life brings me and I live in the moment, knowing that I'll know what I need to know when I need to know it.

My story was made to hold this chapter.

In the present, I am most accessible to Spirit, however I understand it.

Check out the Liminal Playlist to get access to the 7 min guided breathing exercise for this threshold.

Scan To Access

The Ambiguous Middle

The pressure to know, choose, or define.

Threshold Two is not about rebuilding in the traditional sense of the word. It is not about direction or clarity. It is about taking gentle inventory: noticing what remains intact, what has fallen away, what feels unexpectedly tender, what no longer fits, and what still holds you steady even as everything else shifts. This threshold invites you to find your footing. These questions are not meant to rush you forward. They are a life raft to hold onto so you don't slip into the meaninglessness that often shadows this kind of inner unraveling.

Where do you feel pressure (e.g. work, personal, spiritual) to have answers right now, and how does that pressure affect your ability to hear yourself? Pause. Take a deep inhale, then exhale, notice what comes up and begin to express yourself.

What is the hardest part of sitting in uncertainty, and what do you wish the people around you understood about this place you are in?

What do you need right now that you have not allowed yourself to ask for, and what do you imagine might shift if you did?

The Body Compass

When your body becomes the only reliable narrator.

This stage is about helping you recognize your body as a source of wisdom, not a source of overwhelm. It's where somatic intelligence meets spiritual honesty. Because for so many of us, we learned early that discomfort was something to push through. We were taught that duty comes first, and our bodies come second. Rest was often seen as laziness, and fatigue a normal part of doing "good work". So the body became an archive…

What sensations consistently appear in your body during this season of liminality, and what might they be trying to communicate?

How are you trying to care for yourself? Or how might you be ignoring what you need?

When you slow down long enough to feel what is happening inside you, where do you sense:

Relief:

....

....

....

....

Tension:

....

....

....

....

Heaviness:

....

....

....

....

How does your body respond
when you acknowledge it?

Bills and responsibility are real and life rarely gives pauses. How does your body respond when you attempt to make decisions from urgency, fear, or survival, and what does that response reveal about the pace or direction your spirit might need?

How is exhaustion showing up in your body right now, and what is it asking you to stop sustaining?

Expired Maps

What no longer guides you.

Some lessons we carry were never born from wisdom. They were born from fear, scarcity, or the need to keep the peace. We learn to call these lessons prudence, obedience, or good leadership, even when they quiet the voice of our own becoming. This is where you begin to notice the beliefs and expectations that shaped you long after they stopped serving you.

Which beliefs once shaped your decisions but no longer feel true or sustainable?

Which rules once shaped your decisions
but no longer feel true or sustainable?

What have you been taught to call "responsible" or "realistic" that might actually be the language of indoctrination, not imagination?

When you look at the responsibilities you've carried, which ones were fueled more by pressure or obligation than by genuine desire?

Where have you been holding more than your spirit can sustainably carry?

Where in your life have you shaped yourself
around other people's expectations?

What parts of you became fluent in anticipating
the needs of others instead of honoring your own?

ACTIVITY

The Mask

PURPOSE:

To explore the roles, identities, and adaptations you've worn to survive, succeed, or belong — and to notice what no longer fits.

INSTRUCTIONS:

Inside the mask, write down the roles, beliefs, and stories that have shaped your identity but that you feel you are outgrowing — or being asked to retire. Try not to overthink or edit. Let the words flow — even if they feel contradictory.

The Heat of Your Anger

In life, especially for women of color, anger is rarely welcomed as a teacher. We are taught to be composed, gracious, and "above it," even when something inside us is burning with clarity. Anger is often treated as a failure of character rather than a signal of truth. And yet its flame is a constant presence that we are expected to tame for the comfort of others.

In this threshold, anger is not something to correct or suppress. It is information. It often carries the grief of boundaries crossed, needs ignored, or identities compressed to keep the peace.

Where are you carrying anger in this season,
and what does it want you to finally name?

Honoring Your Loss

Grief is not always tied to something concrete or visible. Sometimes it emerges when a chapter is closing, even if the reasons make sense. Sometimes it arrives because something is ending earlier than expected. Other times, because it stayed longer than it should have.

On the pages that follow, give yourself permission to acknowledge what is being lost even if you cannot fully explain it.

Allow yourself to write freely.
Let this be an act of witnessing, not fixing.

Gentle Reorientation

Early signals of what's awakening.

As these long-held patterns loosen their grip,
what faint desires or truths become easier to hear,
even if you are not ready to act on anything?

How does your body respond?

Is there any part of you that feels like it is slowly returning?

What feels different about it now?

When you give yourself permission to slow down,
what patterns rush to push you back into motion?

What fears or assumptions come with that push?

Where do you see evidence that you are getting life right, even if it does not look the way you once imagined?

Closing Activities

After completing this threshold or pausing for the day, complete any *one* of these activities.

Return to these activities as needed.

ACTIVITY ONE

Listening

Sit for 3 minutes without answering anything. Notice what reaches for clarity first — your mind or your body? What thoughts, images or words come to mind? What sensations or emotions feel present in your body? Simply note. No need to figure anything out right now.

ACTIVITY TWO

Statements

Before you move forward, take a moment to empty your hands of any statements, rules or beliefs that are no longer yours to carry.

Then, gently turn your attention to what is waiting to be held.

Let your own interpretation guide you.

Statements I am releasing...	*Statements I am welcoming into my life...*

Threshold Three

NAMING THE LIFE THAT WANTS YOU

Reclaiming imagination, authority, and the courage to create from truth

There is a moment that comes after the dust settles when something begins to stir again. Not loudly. Not confidently. Often quietly enough that you almost miss it. This is not the return of certainty. It is the return of curiosity, desire, imagination, or longing in a body that has learned to survive.

For many, this is the moment where fear becomes louder again. Not because something is wrong, but because imagination has often been labeled irresponsible, immature, or impractical—especially for those who carry businesses, leadership roles, families, financial obligations, and the weight of systems that do not pause for personal transformation.

If you notice your survival instincts activating here, that makes sense. When you begin to imagine differently, part of you will immediately scan for danger. It will ask whether this is practical, whether it is safe, whether now is the wrong time. These questions are not signs that you are regressing. They are signs that you are imagining from within reality, not outside of it.

This threshold is not about escaping the world as it is. You are still living inside systems that have not changed simply because you have. There are political, economic, relational, and structural realities that shape what is possible in any given moment. These are not failures of imagination. They are the landscape you are imagining within.

What matters here is not whether you can change everything. It is whether you can name what is rising honestly, without immediately shutting it down or forcing it into action. Whether you can allow a vision, desire, or truth to exist before you demand certainty from it.

Threshold Three invites you to notice what is asking for expression now. Not what you must build. Not what you must commit to. Simply what feels alive, curious, unfinished, or quietly persistent beneath the fear.

For me, it was a return to my creativity — an aspect of myself I had abandoned in order to achieve a greater sense of security in the world. Writing, painting, sketching, and poetry became a life raft in what felt like an endless sea of uncertainty.

The permission to create came begrudgingly. I had internalized the belief that creativity was a privilege I had not earned. But that awareness exposed a blockage. And addressing that blockage created clarity.

This journal was birthed from that openness.

In the pages that follow, you will be asked to name what is rising while also acknowledging what is out of your control. This is not a contradiction. It is the practice of imagining without bypassing, of honoring truth while staying grounded in the world as it is.

Ground

Before writing, place both feet on the ground.

Take one slow breath in and one slow breath out. Notice what feels alive.

Find a color or image that embodies that aliveness. Collect a swatch and save it here on the page.

Affirm

I choose to remember that I am not what I produce.

I am not the pressure I've survived.

I am not the fear that rises when I dare to dream again.

I release the belief that I must earn ease.

I release the lie that I must suffer to be worthy.

In this season, I will be gentle with myself as I work out effective and sustainable ways to create in the world.

What Is Rising?

Sometimes it's easier to name what you no longer want than to name what you desire. This is especially true after a season of disruption, when imagination has been quiet or overshadowed by responsibility. The questions that follow are not asking you to decide anything or make anything happen. They are simply an invitation to notice what keeps returning, what feels alive, and what is beginning to take shape beneath the uncertainty.

What part of you feels steady or aligned right now, even if everything else still feels uncertain?

What truth about who you are keeps returning to you, even when you have tried to ignore or outrun it?

When you imagine the version of yourself that is rising in this season, what qualities or convictions still feel most aligned?

If no one told you how this desire should come to life, if no one handed you a definition of what a "beautiful" or "successful" life looks like — what would you define for yourself?

ACTIVITY

Naming What Is Rising (Without Words)

If language feels limiting, use the next few facing pages to express what is rising visually. You might collage images, symbols, colors, or shapes.

If visuals feel like too much, simply list words or phrases. No sentences required. Let the words arrive without organizing them.

The Reality It Rises Within

Many ask, "How do I imagine a new way forward when the world feels like it's on fire?". When responsibility, caregiving, leadership, and survival blur together, imagination can feel irresponsible or unrealistic. This work is not about bypassing reality. It is about naming it honestly. There are aspects of your life that are not easily moved right now. These are not failures. They are the conditions you are living within. Use the space below to name the responsibilities, systems, or realities you must currently account for.

What realities or responsibilities are shaping what is possible for you right now?

What Constrains vs. What Can Loosen

As you begin to name what is rising, it's natural for fear to rear its protective head. Some constraints are real and external. Others live quietly inside us as beliefs, excuses, self-imposed responsibilities, or inherited expectations. You and I both know the list can run long. The questions below are not meant to eliminate fear or force clarity. They are here to help you distinguish between what truly cannot be changed in this season and what may be ready to release or shift.

Repeated disappointments or past failures can quietly convince you that you are the problem.

What belief about failure are you ready to define and release?

What meaning about your journey feels more true to claim now?

There are moments when you may feel overlooked by G-d or by life itself. What conversation are you now having with the divine, and how is it shaping what still feels sacred to you?

Life will always hold both beauty and burden.
In this season, how are you practicing self-trust when things feel unfair, unpredictable, or outside your control?

What needs to be healed, released, aligned, or brought into your awareness in order for you to embrace your curiosity and exploratory wisdom?

CLOSING ACTIVITY

One Step Forward

As you close this threshold, ask yourself

"What is one small way I can honor what feels alive in me now?"

Write your response without editing it. This is not a promise. It is an acknowledgment.

Close the journal knowing you do not need the entire path. One honest step is enough.

Threshold Four

CHARTING THE NEW WAY FORWARD

How vision learns to breathe in a real body, in a real world, over time.

There comes a point in the liminal season when something has been named, though it is not yet fully formed. There may be no guarantees, no rewards, and no visible opportunities to mark a breakthrough. What is clear, however, is that old meaning has been dismantled. Your sense of who you are in the world has shifted. What matters most has come into focus, even if the future has not.

This is the threshold where many people feel like they are rebuilding from ground zero. Or expect certainty to arrive.

A clear plan. A defining moment. A timeline. Proof that the rupture or unraveling was worth it. Instead, what often arrives is something quieter and more demanding. The invitation to live from what you know is true before the path ahead is fully visible.

For some, this season brings clarity in subtle ways. Meaning changes shape. Attention sharpens. What once went unnoticed becomes visible. When you allow your understanding of success, fulfillment, or alignment to evolve, you may begin to recognize moments of resonance that would have been easy to overlook before.

This is not to say that breakthroughs, opportunities, or life-changing shifts do not occur. They do, and for some they arrive clearly and quickly. But defining the value of this season by the expectation of a particular outcome can narrow what you are able to receive. Threshold Four is not about finishing the work or bringing a vision to life in an industrialized way. It is about learning how to stay in relationship with what is rising while continuing to live inside real constraints. Responsibilities remain. Bills, relationships, caregiving, work, and the state of the world do not pause because you are changing.

This is why fear often resurfaces here. Not because what is emerging is wrong or unrealistic, but because choosing to live without a template can feel destabilizing. Many of us were taught to trust systems, formulas, and proof over our own timing. This threshold asks you to lead, create, and decide from a newer version of yourself, shaped by values that may not align with the rules you were taught to follow. The old voice often returns at this point, asking for guarantees before permission. It questions the path when results are slow or unclear.

This threshold does not ask you to bypass reality or deny the weight of your circumstances. It asks something more honest. To notice how you respond when certainty is unavailable. To observe where you tighten, rush, overexplain, or abandon yourself in an effort to regain control.

Staying with what is rising does not mean forcing outcomes or acting before you are ready. It means allowing your inner orientation to guide how you move and communicate, even when you cannot yet explain the destination. It means trusting timing without surrendering agency. It means practicing integrity in small, ordinary moments where nothing is resolved and no one is watching.

Threshold Four offers a space to explore how you remain faithful to what you know, even when it has not yet produced visible results. How you choose again, not once but repeatedly, when old patterns call you back. How you learn to live from your truth in ways that are sustainable, grounded, and honest.

Affirm

I trust that what has been placed in me does not require burnout to be birthed.

Even when doubt visits,
Even when I feel unsteady,
I remain connected to what sustains me.

When Fear Is Present, But Not Leading

I often remind myself of two things.

First, new opportunities often present as risks.

Second, when *working through "the wait"*, fearlessness is not the measure of alignment.

These questions are not meant to eliminate fear, but to help you listen without letting it decide for you.

In seasons of transition, fear often reveals where trust is still being cultivated. When you listen to the fears that are present for you now, what is trust asking of you in this season?

Where does the fear of moving in a new way show up
in your body, and what truth becomes louder
when you listen beneath that fear?

Money fears often trigger our survival instincts. How is your definition of "security" changing as you navigate this uncertainty?

When you notice yourself scanning for danger or failure, what happens if you also scan for evidence of support and or alignment?

If fear stepped aside briefly, what desire or possibility would become easier to acknowledge?

Timing and Trusting the Unseen

Sometimes we question our decision to follow what feels true when it does not quickly yield visible results such as money, validation, or traction. As you begin to imagine what comes next, timing becomes its own question. Not everything that is alive in you is meant to be acted on immediately. Some seeds need darkness. Some need moments of quiet exploration. Some seasons ask for rest and isolation rather than sharing and execution. Trusting yourself now includes trusting when to move and when to wait.

Do you trust that you will know what you need to know when the time comes?

What makes this hard or accessible for you?

What signals help you recognize when it is time to move and when it is time to pause?

Where might the fear of getting it wrong be limiting your willingness to explore or experiment?

Leading Without Self-Betrayal

Whether leading yourself, or others, these questions invite you to sit with a central inquiry of this threshold:

What does liberation mean to you in this season, and how might your life or work begin to change if you allowed that truth to lead?

In the spaces where others look to you for guidance, where do you notice yourself performing rather than embodying what you value?

What small shifts can you make to foster greater alignment with what you are trying to welcome into your life?

People-pleasing and hyper-vigilance often begin as mechanisms of protection. What have they protected in your leadership, and what might become possible if you loosen your reliance on them?

Sometimes the hardest part of change is worrying about how others will interpret it. What story are you ready to release about how others interpret your choices, and what story feels more honest now?

Loyalty can be a double-edged sword. What does loyalty mean to you in this season, and how can you honor your growth without abandoning your relationships?

When you stop comparing your path to others,
what becomes clearer about how you want to lead or live?

Sometimes being needed everywhere keeps you from facing where you most need yourself. Where have you been hiding inside responsibility, and what truth becomes clearer when your own needs matter too?

CLOSING ACTIVITY

Anchoring Yourself When Support Is Scarce

Sometimes the people closest to you cannot see what you see. Not out of malice, but because your clarity belongs to you first. When outside affirmation is limited, your connection to yourself becomes essential.

Take a few moments to create a simple grounding plan you can return to when support feels scarce.

1. Name one practice that brings you back into your body. This could be a breath, a quiet pause, a five minute walk, or placing a hand on your heart.

2. Name one practice that helps you hear your intuition. This could be prayer, journaling, silence, or paying attention to the first honest thought that rises.

3. Name one statement you want to remember when others do not understand your decisions. A sentence that steadies you and helps you stay aligned with what you know is true.

Keep this grounding plan somewhere you can return to often. This is how you protect your clarity when the world around you has not caught up yet.

Prayers

These prayers are offered as companions, not prescriptions. You are invited to read them, adapt them, rewrite them, or sit with them quietly. Use the language that feels true for you. Leave what does not.

Prayer, in this context, is not about surrendering agency. It is about remembering that you are not walking alone.

PRAYER 1

All-loving Spirit, pour through my life
a flood of Divine love.

May that love wash my heart clean of
selfishness and self-doubt.

Grant me new sight, that I may see You in all.

May I look to You for joy and sustenance.

May I never grow weary in seeking You,
and may my vision remain clear
and unwavering.

PRAYER 2

Lord, still all turbulence in my heart.

PRAYER 3

Dearest Divine,
I know that I am being shaped and refined
And I am tired.
And I am afraid.

My heart is heavy.
I feel lost.
I am struggling to find my fight.

I do not know what the universe has in store
for me, so I seek your guidance
at this moment.

Grant me the strength to endure
this journey of evolution.
Speak light into my grief, and into the places
where guilt and anger have begun to harden.

Let this growth bring a renewed sense of self,
clarity, and confidence.
Allow your love to reach me through
supportive friendships and quiet,
restorative moments.

Above all, guide me in releasing beliefs that bind
me to a version of myself rooted in fear,
a version that sees only my inadequacies.

In this moment, I am present.
In this moment, I am cared for.
In this moment, I am yours.

PRAYER 4

*All-pervading Deity, help me never to forget
that I am a child of Divinity.*

*May I speak only what is worthy
of a child of G-d.*

*May I think only what is worthy
of a child of G-d.*

May I do only what is worthy of a child of G-d.

*May my life move in harmony with
Your universal Life.*

PRAYER 5

May my heart be open and protected.

May discernment show me what is for me, and what is not.

May I hand back what belongs to others with ease.

May I know my body's yes and no, and listen sooner.

May I remember how safe I am to let things be good.

May it be so.